INTERFACT REFERENCE

SPACE

TWO CAN™

PRINCETON ▪ LONDON

What's in the book?

What's on the disk?

You'll find a whole universe to explore! When you open the disk, you'll meet Captain Collins — your guide to space. Captain Collins will tell you how to use the disk and how to keep track of your progress in your own personal Data Station. Then, go exploring! Exciting activities are hidden in different parts of the universe (see right).

There are seven exciting activities for you to find!

Installing the Space CD-ROM

See page 48 for troubleshooting tips, system requirements, and helpline details.

Windows 95 or 98

The Space program should start automatically when you put the CD into your CD-ROM drive. If it does not, follow these instructions.
1. Put the CD into the CD drive.
2. Double-click on My Computer.
3. Double-click on the CD drive icon.
4. Double-click on the SPACE icon.

Windows 3.1 or 3.11
1. Put the CD into the CD Drive.
2. Open File Manager.
3. Double-click on the CD drive icon.
4. Double-click on the SPACE icon.

Macintosh
1. Put the CD into the CD drive.
2. Double-click on the SPACE FOR MAC icon.

Power Macintosh
1. Put the CD into the CD drive.
2. Double-click on the SPACE FOR POWER MAC icon.

Cosmic Challenge

Meet the one and only Larry Lunar, the host of this challenging game show. Pick the character that you'd like to be, then take your chances against the opponent of your choice!

Liftoff

Here's your chance to build a rocket! All the pieces you'll need are on screen. Once you put the pieces in place, click on the launch button to see if your rocket gets off the ground.

Star Gazing

Would you like to be an astronomer? Using the book to help you, put the pieces of the night sky into place. Then, use your mouse to explore the night sky and learn all about the stars and constellations.

Galactic Gallery

Visit the Galactic Gallery. You'll need to wake up Gerald, the friendly guard, from his afternoon nap. Then he'll help you learn all about distant galaxies and play a fun memory game, too.

Space Academy

Have you ever wondered what it would be like to be an astronaut? Well, here's your chance to find out! Try this interactive adventure and see if you have what it takes to travel into space!

Earth Alert

Emergency! A massive asteroid is plummeting toward Earth. If you're smart, you'll destroy the asteroid before it hits Earth! Just answer the quiz questions as they appear on screen.

Toolbar

The toolbar appears whenever you move the cursor to the right-hand edge of the screen.

Click here to return to the main screen.

Click here to see your Data Station.

Click here to collect your prizes.

Click here to use the glossary.

Click here to use your notebook.

Click here for help.

Click here to quit.

Solar System Mission

It's time to get to work. You are employed by Orbital, the biggest and best trucking company in the solar system. You'll get to travel to every planet in the solar system — but watch out for dangers along the way!

Glossary

Have a problem with a space word that's been used in the book or on the disk? Then look it up in the glossary! Use your toolbar to find this disk feature. It will certainly help you come to terms with all the space terminology!

What is space?

Space is the near emptiness surrounding Earth. It stretches farther than astronomers can see, even with their most powerful telescopes. In space, there are stars, **moons**, galaxies, and **planets**, including Earth. Between the planets and stars, there are tiny bits of dust and **gas**. There may also be other things waiting to be discovered. Everything in space is part of the **universe**.

▶ Scientists think that the universe was formed about 10 to 20 **billion** years ago. These pictures show you what may have happened.

1 Nearly all scientists believe that the universe probably began with a huge explosion that scientists call the big bang. Immediately after the big bang, the universe was small and very hot.

Big Bang

2 Then the universe cooled down and became larger. Huge swirls of dust and gas clung together to make galaxies.

Galaxy

Nebula

3 Inside the galaxies, there were smaller dust and gas clouds called nebulae. This is where the stars were born. One of these stars was the sun. It was born in a galaxy called the Milky Way.

Earth

Mercury

Sun

Venus

Solar system

Uranus

Mars

Jupiter

Saturn

Neptune

Pluto

4 Nine planets formed around the new sun to make the solar system. One of these planets was Earth.

Go to Rocky planet page 30, Sun page 26

Earth

Earth is a huge ball of rock traveling through space. It is one of nine **planets** that **orbit** the sun, and it formed about 4½ billion years ago. Earth is different from the other planets because much of its surface is covered with water. It is also the only planet known to have life. It is home to many kinds of plants and animals. These things can live here because Earth is just the right distance from the sun, making it neither too hot nor too cold.

▼ Below are the different layers that make up Earth.

Crust
The crust is Earth's top, rocky layer. It makes up all the land and the ocean floor.

Mantle
Beneath the crust is a thick layer of hot rock called the mantle.

Outer core
Hot, melted iron forms Earth's outer **core**.

Day and night
Earth spins around like a top. As it spins, only one side faces the sun. The side facing the sun has daytime and the side facing away has nighttime.

Daytime

Earth

Sun

Nighttime

Life on Earth

Three to four **billion** years ago, early forms of life appeared in the ocean. They were too small to see, but they slowly developed into plants, jellyfish, and fish.

About 360 million years ago, some fish began to change and spend part of their time on land. Later, they began to live on land all the time.

Around 230 million years ago, enormous dinosaurs roamed Earth. Suddenly, about 160 million years later, they were all wiped out.

Above Earth

The air around Earth forms its **atmosphere**. Air is made up of several **gases**, including **oxygen**. Below, you can see the different layers of the atmosphere. As you move away from Earth, there is increasingly less air in the atmosphere, until it disappears completely.

1,000 miles...............
(1,600 km)
Space begins where there is no air left.

..........50-300 miles (80-480 km)
A space shuttle flies at 124 miles (200 km) above Earth. There is hardly any air there.

.................30-50 miles (48-80 km)
Here, the air burns up tiny rocks from space to make meteors, or shooting stars.

.........Ozone layer
Some of the sun's rays can be harmful. A gas called ozone helps to stop these rays from reaching Earth.

..........6-30 miles (10-48 km)
Some jet planes fly in this layer of the atmosphere above the clouds.

............0-6 miles (0-10 km)
Close to Earth, there is plenty of air. Most of the clouds are here.

.Inner core
At the Earth's center, the inner core is a hot ball of **solid** iron.

Factfile

It may reach 13,000 °F (7,000 °C) at the Earth's center. That's over 100 times hotter than the hottest desert.

The Earth measures 24,902 miles (40,075 kilometers) around its widest part. It would take 1½ years to walk all the way around.

*Sometimes hot rock from inside Earth bursts out of the crust to form a **volcano**.*

About 140 million years ago, the first birds appeared on the Earth. They had claws on their wings and probably developed from flying reptiles.

Humans have lived on Earth for about two million years. This is a short time compared with the dinosaurs. They lived on Earth about 80 times longer.

Go to Galaxy page 42, Telescope page 10

Astronomer

Astronomers are people who study objects in space, such as the sun, moon, stars, and **planets**. They try to determine what these things are made of, where they are, and how fast they are traveling. Many objects in space are so far away that astronomers need to use powerful telescopes to study them properly. Astronomers are always searching the skies for new discoveries and trying to see farther into space than before.

Copernicus
Over 450 years ago, in 1543, a Polish astronomer called Copernicus suggested that all the planets, including Earth, traveled around the sun. At the time, most other astronomers did not believe him. They could see the sun move across the sky, so they believed that the sun and the planets traveled around Earth. Today, we know that these astronomers were wrong and that Copernicus's ideas were right.

The first astronomers
Long ago, the first astronomers used the movements of the sun, moon, stars, and planets to help people plan their daily lives. Astronomers built towers, such as the one above, to watch the sky. By looking at the different positions of objects in the sky, they could tell when the seasons were about to change and would estimate the best time for farmers to plant their seeds. They could also tell the time by watching the sun move across the sky during the day.

The wrong way
In Picture A, the sun and the planets travel around Earth, so Earth is at the center of the **universe**.

A

Earth

Sun

The right way
Picture B shows you how the planets really travel. Here the sun is at the center and Earth and the other planets travel around it.

B

Sun

Earth

Galileo

Over 350 years ago, in 1610, an Italian astronomer named Galileo discovered that the planet Jupiter had four **moons** circling around it. This proved that everything did not travel around Earth. It made people realize that Copernicus's ideas were right. In this picture you can see two of the telescopes Galileo used to make his discoveries.

Newton

The English scientist Isaac Newton was born about 350 years ago in 1642. According to a story, he watched an apple drop from a tree and wondered why it fell straight to the ground. Then he realized that Earth was pulling everything toward it. He called this **gravity**. Newton also determined why the planets traveled around the sun and did not shoot off in all directions into space. He realized that the sun's gravity pulled the planets and kept them in their paths around the sun.

Modern astronomers

Today, many astronomers work in a control room with computers, such as the one below. They point a telescope at the sky and use it to make pictures of distant stars and galaxies. Computers then add colors to the pictures to make them clearer.

Adding color

A computer has added colors to this picture of a galaxy. The brightest parts are colored white.

Go to Astronomer page 8, Galaxy page 42, Space shuttle page 20

Telescope

A telescope is a tool that astronomers use to find out about space. It makes distant things, such as stars and **planets**, look bigger and nearer. Over 350 years ago, an Italian astronomer named Galileo became the first person to study the night sky with a telescope. Today, telescopes are more powerful than Galileo's and astronomers can see much farther into space.

Tube
Light from stars and planets enters the telescope tube.

Eyepiece................
An astronomer looks through the eyepiece.

Simple telescope
People who study the stars at home often look through a simple telescope, such as the one on the left. Sometimes a camera is fitted to the telescope. It can take photographs that show more detail than the eye can see.

Light

Eyepiece

Mirror

How a telescope works
A curved mirror inside the tube collects light from stars and planets and makes a picture, or image, of part of the sky. An eyepiece makes this image look bigger.

Stand..............
A stand keeps the telescope steady.

Observatory
Large modern telescopes are often built on mountaintops where the sky is clear. Several telescopes are usually grouped together at a place called an observatory. Each telescope is inside a dome-shaped building. A slit in the dome opens to let the telescope point at the sky and take photographs that an astronomer can study. The dome turns around so that the telescope can point at any part of the sky.

Radio telescope

Many objects in space, such as distant galaxies, give out **radio waves**. Astronomers collect these waves with radio telescopes, which look like large dishes. A group of telescopes works together, using the radio waves to make a picture of the object in space. The radio telescopes in this photograph are part of the Very Large Array Telescope in New Mexico, which has 27 dishes linked together.

Hubble Space Telescope

There is a telescope in space that circles around Earth. It is named after the astronomer Edwin Hubble, and it was **launched** in 1990 by the space shuttle. Hubble can see farther than larger telescopes on Earth. This is because in space there are no clouds, or moving air to blur its view. Hubble has taken photographs of many distant stars and galaxies.

Mirror
Inside the tube, a large mirror collects light from stars and galaxies to make pictures.

Cover
A cover stops bright sunlight from entering and harming the telescope.

Solar panel
The solar panels make **electricity** from sunlight to keep the telescope working.

Antenna
The antenna sends down radio-wave messages to Earth

Go to Astronaut page 16, Rocket page 14, Solar system page 28, Sun page 26

Moon

The moon is a ball of rock that circles around Earth about once every 27 days. The same side of the moon, called the nearside, always faces Earth. The other side, called the farside, is hidden from Earth. The moon is the only place in space that astronauts have visited. Twelve astronauts have landed there to explore its surface and bring back rocks. They discovered that the moon was dry and dusty and that nothing lived there.

Surface
The moon's surface is covered with thousands of **craters**. They were made millions of years ago, when rocks from space crashed into the moon.

Crater
A crater has a ring of mountains around its edges. Sometimes there are also mountains in the middle of a crater.

Mountain
Long lines of mountains run across some parts of the moon. These mountains are called the Apennines.

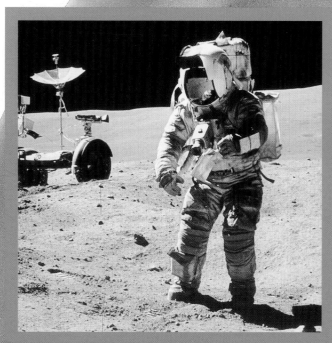

Moon walking
This astronaut is collecting rocks. He has to wear a spacesuit to breathe because there is no air on the moon. His footprints will remain there for thousands of years because there is neither wind nor rain to erase them.

Streak
These streaks on the moon's surface were made when melted rock was flung out of a newly formed crater.

Moon

Earth

Sun

Moonlight

The moon looks bright at night, but it does not make its own light. Instead, the sun shines on the moon, lighting up one side. On moonlit nights, people are really seeing sunlight that has bounced off the moon and down toward Earth.

Factfile

In the sunlight, the moon is twice as hot as the hottest desert on Earth, but in the dark, it is almost twice as cold as the coldest place on Earth.

*In 1959, a Russian **spacecraft** called Luna 3 sent the first pictures of the farside of the moon back to Earth.*

*The moon is bigger than the smallest **planet**, which is Pluto.*

Sea

Each large dark patch on the moon is called a sea. But there is no water on the moon, so the seas are dry.

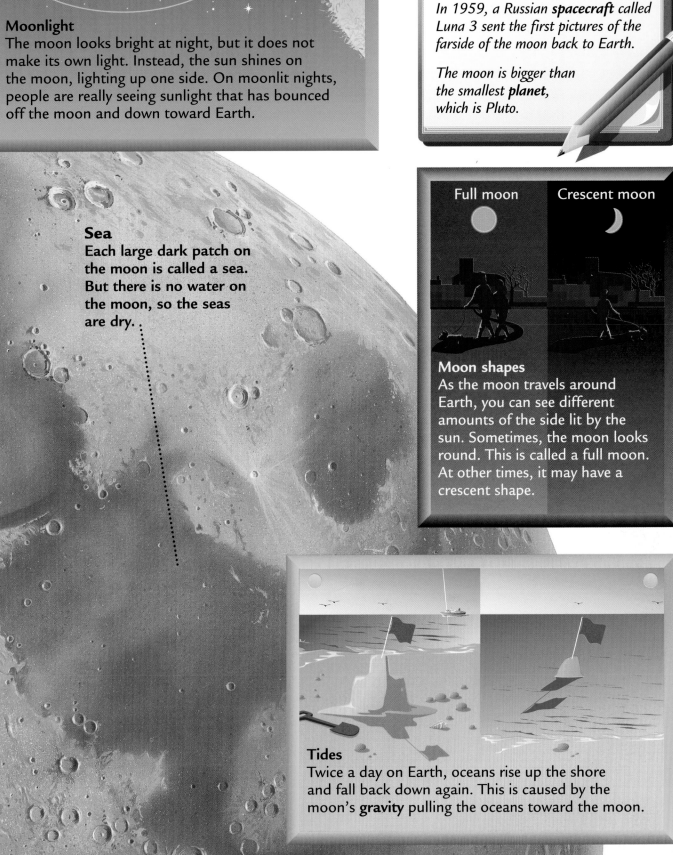

Full moon   Crescent moon

Moon shapes

As the moon travels around Earth, you can see different amounts of the side lit by the sun. Sometimes, the moon looks round. This is called a full moon. At other times, it may have a crescent shape.

Tides

Twice a day on Earth, oceans rise up the shore and fall back down again. This is caused by the moon's **gravity** pulling the oceans toward the moon.

Go to Astronaut page 16, Moon page 12, Satellite page 22

Rocket

A rocket is a **vehicle** that can carry astronauts or satellites into space. It has powerful **engines** that burn **fuel**, pushing it up into the sky. Most rockets have two or three sections, called stages. Each stage has its own engines and fuel. The stages burn up their fuel one at a time and then drop away. This makes the rocket lighter, letting it travel faster and faster until it reaches space.

Escape rocket
An escape rocket could carry the astronauts away if something went wrong

Apollo spacecraft
The astronauts traveled to the moon inside the Apollo **spacecraft**.

Third stage
The third stage provided extra power to send the astronauts to the moon.

Saturn V
Saturn V was one of the most powerful types of rockets ever built. Between 1968 and 1972, it was used for the Apollo missions to take astronauts to the moon. Five main engines lifted the rocket off the **launch pad** until it was traveling 350 times faster than a car on a highway.

Second stage
The second stage was smaller than the first stage. It lifted the astronauts into space.

First stage
Inside the first stage, there were two large tanks that held the fuel for the five main engines.

Engine
The five main engines were at the bottom of the rocket.

Crawler
This crawler carried the rocket to the launch pad. It moved so slowly that a person could walk to the launch pad faster than it could crawl there.

14

To the moon and back

During an Apollo mission, three astronauts traveled to the moon in the small Apollo spacecraft, but only two of them landed. One astronaut stayed in the spacecraft, circling the moon, while the other two flew down to the surface in the **lunar lander**. The astronauts came back to Earth in the part of the spacecraft shown on the right. They landed in the sea and were picked up by a ship waiting nearby.

Ariane

Ariane is a type of rocket that launches satellites. Astronauts do not travel on board. The rocket is controlled from Earth by scientists.

7 The satellite at the top of the third stage is carried higher. It is then released into **orbit** around Earth.

6 The second stage drops away, leaving only the third stage and the satellite.

5 The covers that protect the satellite are thrown off.

4 The second stage engines start firing to push the rest of the rocket up.

3 When the first stage has used up its fuel, it drops away as well.

2 The **booster rockets** soon use up their fuel and fall away into the sea.

1 The Ariane rocket blasts off, carrying its satellite into space.

Astronaut

Astronauts are men and women who travel in space to explore such places as the moon or to carry out experiments. They also repair **machines**, such as telescopes and satellites. There is no air in space, so when astronauts leave their **spacecraft**, they must wear **spacesuits** that provide them with air to breathe. Astronauts have to train for a long time before they are ready to travel into space.

Astronaut training

Floating in a water tank helps teach an astronaut how it feels to be **weightless**.

In space, there is no right way up. A spinning chair helps an astronaut imagine how this feels.

An astronaut learns how to fly a spacecraft by studying its flight controls.

Cooling tube
It can become hot inside a spacesuit, so tubes pump cool water around the suit to cool down the astronaut.

Pocket
An astronaut's spacesuit has pockets on it that hold small tools.

Astronaut's glove
These special gloves screw on the spacesuit. They let the astronaut's fingers bend to do work.

Cable
A cable joins the astronaut to the spacecraft. It stops the astronaut from floating away when working outside the spacecraft.

Moon landing
Astronauts have landed on the moon six times. On some missions, they used the moon buggy, shown on the right of the photograph, to explore new areas away from the landing site.

Chest pack
An astronaut wears a chest pack in front. It has controls for the spacesuit and tells the astronaut if anything is wrong.

Visor
In space, the sun is very bright, so an astronaut wears a gold visor to protect the eyes.

Microphone
This microphone lies underneath the astronaut's helmet and enables the astronaut to talk to people back in the spacecraft.

Factfile

The first woman to travel into space was Valentina Tereshkova, a Soviet cosmonaut. She spent almost three days in space in 1963.

In March 1965, Soviet cosmonaut Alexei Leonov became the first person to spacewalk outside his spacecraft.

The word astronaut *means* star traveler.

Space station

A space station is a home in space. Astronauts live here and carry out experiments to learn more about how space affects people. Inside the space station, there is air to breathe, so the astronauts do not need to wear spacesuits. In 1986, Russia **launched** a new space station called Mir. Rockets brought up the station's different parts and joined them together in space.

▶ **Mir space station**

Control desk
Astronauts control the space station from here.

Solar panel
These panels use the sun's rays to make **electricity**, which provides power for the space station.

Living quarters
Astronauts sleep, eat, and work in the living quarters. This was the first part of Mir to be launched into space.

Factfile

In 1995, Russian Valery Polyakov set a record for the longest time spent in space – 438 days.

In 1993, Russia and the United States agreed to build a combined space station called the International Space Station. Unity and Zarya, launched in 1998, are its first two units.

Astronauts stand in a big bag to take a shower. A tube sucks away the water when they have finished washing.

Astronauts must drink through straws to stop any liquids from floating away. They eat food that comes in closed foil packets.

Manned Maneuvering Unit
Astronauts sometimes wear a **machine** called a Manned Maneuvering Unit (MMU) to move around when making repairs in space.

Storage
The MMU is stored in this part of the space station.

Space shuttle
A space shuttle takes astronauts to and from the space station.

Docking bay
Visiting **spacecraft** join the space station at the docking bay.

Astronauts use the MMU to move about. They push levers that let off **gas** to go backward and forward and to turn around.

Astronauts need to exercise to keep themselves fit. They spend half an hour each day on exercise bikes to stop their muscles from becoming weak.

Astronauts can sleep standing up. They are strapped in sleeping bags attached to the wall. They wear earplugs to block out noise.

Go to Astronaut page 16, Satellite page 22, Space probe page 24, Space station page 18, Telescope page 10

Space shuttle

A space shuttle is a special plane that can fly into space and back to Earth many times. It can take astronauts to a space station or launch a satellite or space probe. A shuttle has several parts. The part that carries the astronauts is called the shuttle orbiter. The other parts are a huge **fuel** tank and two **booster rockets**. The fuel tank is the only part of the space shuttle that cannot be used again.

Take off and landing

1 The shuttle takes off like a rocket, using its three main engines. It gets extra power from the two booster rockets.

2 When the fuel from the boosters is used up, they fall into the sea. The large fuel tank will fall away too.

3 The shuttle orbiter lands with its engines switched off. It glides down to the runway on Earth like an airplane.

▼ **Space shuttle orbiter**

Payload bay
Cameras and telescopes in the payload bay take pictures of Earth or study the stars in space.

Tile
When the shuttle comes back to Earth, it becomes very hot. Thousands of special tiles stop it from burning up.

Engine
The three main engines are not used in space. Smaller engines move the shuttle and take it back toward Earth.

Payload bay door
In space, the doors of the payload bay are open to let extra heat from the cabin escape.

Spacelab
Spacelab is a **laboratory** where the astronauts work. The shuttle carries the lab within its payload bay.

Robot arm
The robot arm can launch or capture a satellite. Astronauts can attach themselves to the arm to make repairs to the satellite.

Cabin
On the upper deck of the cabin, there are controls for flying the shuttle. The astronauts eat, sleep, and work on a deck below.

Tunnel
An astronaut floats through a tunnel to move from the shuttle cabin to Spacelab.

Factfile

There are four shuttle orbiters. They are called Columbia, Atlantis, Discovery, and Endeavour.

On January 28, 1986, the shuttle Challenger exploded 73 seconds after takeoff, killing all seven astronauts on board.

During takeoff, the power of a shuttle's engines is the same as 140 jumbo jets.

Into space
In April 1990, the Hubble Space Telescope was launched by the space shuttle Discovery. An astronaut in the shuttle cabin worked the controls for the robot arm, which put the telescope into **orbit**.

Satellite

A satellite is a **machine** that circles around Earth. There are many kinds of satellites, and they do different jobs. Some study the weather or Earth's surface, and others send messages from one part of the world to another. Satellites have different **orbits** depending on the job they do. Powerful rockets carry the satellites up into space and put them into the right orbit.

▶ These are four of the satellites **orbiting** around Earth.

Navstar
A satellite, such as Navstar, helps ships and planes find their way, or navigate.

Meteosat
Meteosat is a weather satellite. It monitors the clouds and measures the strength of the wind. It also sends to Earth information on the **temperature** of the land, sea, and air.

A television forecaster uses the measurements from a weather satellite to tell people what the weather will be like over several days.

Messages sent by Navstar tell a captain where his ship is, even in bad weather. They can also tell him how fast the ship is traveling.

Satellite pictures from Landsat are studied by scientists. They can show how well crops are growing, spot forest fires, and b used to make maps of Earth.

Intelsat
Intelsat is a communications satellite. It collects television and telephone signals from one place on Earth and sends them back down to another place.

Landsat
Some satellites, such as Landsat, look down at Earth. They send back pictures of forests, farmland, and **pollution** in the sea and air.

A telephone conversation may travel up to a communications satellite and then down to someone on the end of a phone in another country.

A communications satellite sends television programs from one country to another, so people all over the world can watch them.

Factfile

In 1957, Russia launched Sputnik 1, which was the world's first satellite. It circled the Earth in just over 1½ hours.

In 1990, there were about 2,000 working satellites orbiting Earth.

The first weather satellite to send pictures of clouds back to Earth was called Tiros. It was launched in April 1960.

Go to Comet and asteroid page 34, Gas planet page 32, Rocky planet page 30

Space probe

A space probe is a **machine** that explores space and sends information and pictures back to Earth. Astronauts do not travel in a space probe. Instead, it is controlled by scientists on the ground. Some probes are launched by a rocket, others by a space shuttle. Probes have visited many **moons** and all the **planets** except Pluto. They have sent back information about the weather, **temperature,** and surface of these places.

Neptune

Uranus

Dark spot
In 1989, a space probe found a dark spot on the planet Neptune. It was a huge storm about the size of Earth, but it now seems to have disappeared.

Voyager 2
space probe

Saturn

Jupiter

Voyager
In 1977, two space probes called Voyager 1 and 2 set out to visit the giant planets farthest away from the sun. Both probes flew past Jupiter and Saturn, and Voyager 2 also went on to visit Uranus and Neptune. The probes sent back pictures of the planets' moons and surfaces. The Voyagers' radio receivers and magnetism detectors were still operating in the

Viking

In 1976, two probes named Viking reached the planet Mars. The probes circled around Mars, making maps of its surface, while **landers** traveled to the ground. These landers tested rocks and soil to see if anything lived there, but they found nothing. You can see a Viking lander below. In 1996, more probes were sent to explore other parts of Mars.

Magellan

The Magellan space probe arrived at Venus in 1990. It could not take photographs because thick clouds hid the planet's surface. Instead, it bounced **radio waves** off the planet. Computers on Earth were then able to make pictures from these radio waves. This picture shows mountains and **volcanoes** on Venus's surface. The dark parts are the places that Magellan missed.

Galileo

The most recent probe to visit Jupiter is called Galileo. It arrived in 1995, after a six-year journey. The main probe dropped a smaller probe, shown on the right, by parachute into Jupiter's clouds. For nearly an hour, it sent information about the clouds up to the main probe and then back to scientists waiting on Earth. The main probe then circled around Jupiter and visited its four large moons.

Jupiter

small probe

Ida

The Galileo space probe sent back the first ever close-up photographs of space rocks, or asteroids. It saw this one, called Ida, on its way to Jupiter.

Go to Earth page 6, Moon page 12, Solar system page 28, Star page 36

Sun

The sun is a huge fiery ball of **gas** that glows in the sky. It is the closest star to Earth. Like all stars, the sun gives out **energy** as heat and light. Much of this is lost in space but some of it reaches Earth. Without heat and light, Earth would be dark and cold and nothing could live here.

Warming Earth

The sun always warms Earth, but it shines more strongly on some places than on others. At Earth's far north and south, the sun shines weakly, so the land is always cold. At Earth's middle, the sun shines strongly. There, it is always warm.

Using sunlight

The panels on the roof of this house use sunlight to make **electricity**, which runs such **machines** as a stove and a television.

Flare
Sometimes hot gas bursts out of the sun as a flare.

Prominence
A prominence is a huge tongue or loop of gas that rises high above the sun's surface.

WARNING!
Never look directly at the sun. Its light is so bright that it will harm your eyes.

Corona
The corona is the name of the layer of thin gas all around the sun.

Sun's surface
Hot gas bubbles up on the sun's surface and glows yellow.

Core
The **core** is where the sun makes its energy.

Factfile

Light from the sun travels almost 93 million miles (150 million km) to reach Earth. It would take a car over 200 years to travel this far, but it takes light only eight minutes.

An ancient Chinese legend explained an eclipse as a dragon eating the sun.

The sun spins around once every 27 days.

Sunspot
Dark patches on the sun are called sunspots. These areas are cooler than the rest of the sun's surface.

Under the sun's surface
Here, churning gas carries energy to the surface of the sun where it can escape.

Moon   Sun

Earth

Eclipse
As the moon travels around Earth, it can pass directly between Earth and the sun. When this happens, the sun is completely hidden for a few minutes. This is an eclipse of the sun.

Ring of light
During an eclipse of the sun, the moon blocks out most of the sun's light. Only the pale glow of the sun's corona can be seen.

Solar system

The solar system is the name given to the sun
and all the objects in space that travel around it.
In the solar system, there are nine **planets** and their
moons, comets, and chunks of rock called asteroids
and meteoroids. The planets lie huge distances apart
and take different lengths of time to travel
around the sun. The time it takes for a
planet to circle the sun once is called
its year. The planets also spin
around like tops. The time it
takes for a planet to
spin around once
is its day.

▼ The planets are the largest
objects in the solar system
except for the sun.

Jupiter
Jupiter is larger than
all the other planets
put together.

Mars
Mars is about
half the size of
Earth and much
colder.

Moon

Earth
Earth is the third
planet from the sun.
Many different plants
and animals live here.

sun

Venus
Venus is the
nearest planet
to Earth, and
almost the
same size.

Mercury
The only planet
smaller than
Mercury is
Pluto.

28

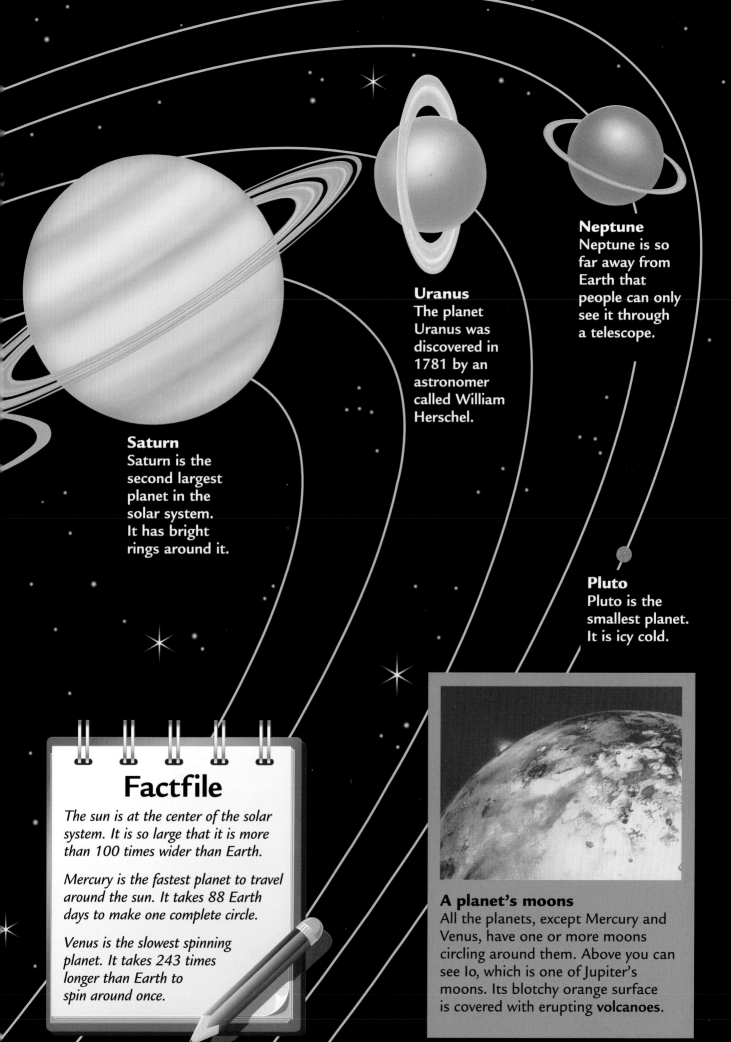

Saturn
Saturn is the second largest planet in the solar system. It has bright rings around it.

Uranus
The planet Uranus was discovered in 1781 by an astronomer called William Herschel.

Neptune
Neptune is so far away from Earth that people can only see it through a telescope.

Pluto
Pluto is the smallest planet. It is icy cold.

Factfile

The sun is at the center of the solar system. It is so large that it is more than 100 times wider than Earth.

Mercury is the fastest planet to travel around the sun. It takes 88 Earth days to make one complete circle.

Venus is the slowest spinning planet. It takes 243 times longer than Earth to spin around once.

A planet's moons
All the planets, except Mercury and Venus, have one or more moons circling around them. Above you can see Io, which is one of Jupiter's moons. Its blotchy orange surface is covered with erupting **volcanoes**.

Go to Earth page 6, Solar system page 28, Space probe page 24

Rocky planet

A rocky **planet** is made up of rock and metal. It has a rocky surface with a metal **core**. The four planets nearest the sun, which are Mercury, Venus, Earth, and Mars, are all rocky planets. Pluto, the planet farthest away from the sun, is similar to them, but its core is made of rock instead of metal. Pluto is so cold that its surface is covered with a thick layer of ice.

Crashing into Venus

This crater was made by a rock that hit Venus. All the rocky planets in the solar system have craters on their surface.

Venus

Venus is nearly the same size as Earth but it would not be a good planet for astronauts to visit because it is surrounded by thick, poisonous clouds. These clouds keep Venus even hotter than Mercury, although it is farther away from the sun. The air on Venus presses down so hard that space probes have been crushed when they landed there.

Crust

The outer layer, or crust, of Venus is made of rock.

Mercury

Mercury looks similar to the moon. It is covered with thousands of **craters** that formed when rocks from space crashed into it millions of years ago. The side of Mercury that faces the sun is over seven times hotter than the hottest desert on Earth. The side facing away from the sun is extremely cold. There is no air or water on Mercury.

Surface

Venus has mountains, craters, and **volcanoes** on its surface.

Core

The core of Venus is made of a metal called iron.

Canyon

.... Olympus Mons

Two moons
Mars has two small rocky **moons**, that are shaped like potatoes and covered with craters. This is the larger moon called Phobos. The smaller moon is called Deimos.

On the surface
Rust-colored sand and rocks lie on the surface of Mars.

Mars
Mars is a dry and dusty planet. Its winds whip up huge dust storms that make its sky look pink. Large deserts, deep **canyons,** and giant volcanoes cover Mars. The biggest volcano in the solar system is there. Its name is Olympus Mons. Mars is called the red planet because from the Earth it looks red in the sky.

Pluto
Pluto is a tiny planet right at the edge of the solar system. It is so small and far away that astronomers do not know much about it. Pluto was discovered in 1930. Then, in 1978, astronomers found that it had a moon, which they named Charon. This is how Pluto and Charon might look from a visiting **spacecraft.**

Traveling around
Pluto takes 248 Earth years to travel once around the sun. Its path crosses with the planet Neptune, but there is little danger that they will hit each other.

Sun

Neptune

Pluto

Charon

Pluto

Planet X
A few astronomers think there may be another planet, which they call Planet X, that may be even farther away from us than Pluto. They are watching space probes speeding out of the solar system to see if they can find this new planet. These probes have now passed Pluto, but there has been no sign of Planet X yet.

Go to Astronomer page 8, Solar system page 28, Space probe page 24

Gas planet

A gas **planet** is made up mostly of **gases** and **liquids**. It has a rocky **core** that is covered in a thick layer of liquid or ice. On the outside of a gas planet, there are layers of colored clouds. Jupiter, Saturn, Uranus, and Neptune are gas planets. If astronauts ever manage to visit these distant places, they would not be able to explore them on foot, because there is no hard surface on which a **spacecraft** could land.

Clouds · Liquid

· Metal-like liquid

· Core

Inside Jupiter
Jupiter is made up of four different layers. At the center, there is a small, rocky core. Then, there are two layers of liquid. Jupiter's surface is made up of red and yellow swirling clouds.

Jupiter
The biggest planet in the solar system is Jupiter. Measuring across the middle, it is more than 11 times larger than the Earth. Jupiter spins faster than any other planet too. It is also very bright, which makes it easy to spot in the night sky. Venus is the only planet in the solar system that is brighter.

All the gas planets have rings around them. Jupiter's ring is so thin that it is difficult to see.

The red and white spots in Jupiter's clouds are storms. The largest of these storms is called the Great Red Spot. It is bigger than planet Earth and has lasted for at least 300 years.

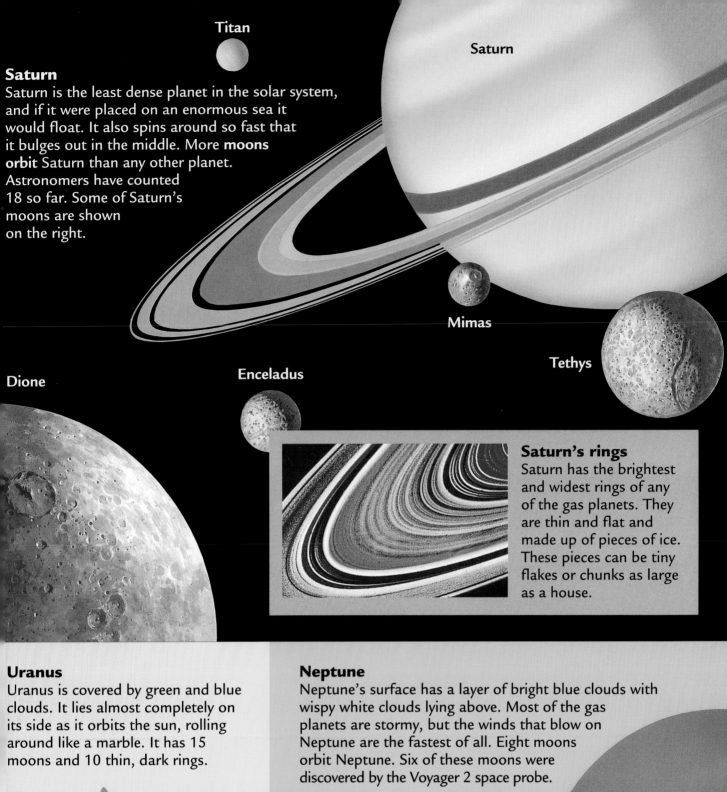

Titan

Saturn

Saturn is the least dense planet in the solar system, and if it were placed on an enormous sea it would float. It also spins around so fast that it bulges out in the middle. More **moons orbit** Saturn than any other planet. Astronomers have counted 18 so far. Some of Saturn's moons are shown on the right.

Mimas

Tethys

Dione

Enceladas

Saturn's rings

Saturn has the brightest and widest rings of any of the gas planets. They are thin and flat and made up of pieces of ice. These pieces can be tiny flakes or chunks as large as a house.

Uranus

Uranus is covered by green and blue clouds. It lies almost completely on its side as it orbits the sun, rolling around like a marble. It has 15 moons and 10 thin, dark rings.

Neptune

Neptune's surface has a layer of bright blue clouds with wispy white clouds lying above. Most of the gas planets are stormy, but the winds that blow on Neptune are the fastest of all. Eight moons orbit Neptune. Six of these moons were discovered by the Voyager 2 space probe.

Triton

Triton is Neptune's largest moon and the coldest known place in the solar system.

Comet and asteroid

Comets and asteroids are part of the solar system. Like **planets** and **moons**, they travel around the sun. Comets are made of dust and ice and look like dirty snowballs. Astronomers think there are millions of them traveling through space. Asteroids are chunks of rock. The biggest asteroids are hundreds of miles wide but most are as small as pebbles.

A comet's path
A comet travels from the edge of the solar system toward the sun. It then swings around the sun and heads away again.

A comet's tail
A comet is too small to see from Earth, except when it comes close to the sun. Then the sun's heat melts some of the comet's ice, making a huge cloud of dust and **gas**. This streams into a long tail, which is sometimes bright enough to see in the night sky. The tail of the comet points away from the sun.

Head
The icy center of a comet is hidden inside its head, under a glowing dust cloud.

Tail
A comet's tail can be 100 million miles (160 million kilometers) long.

Halley's comet
Halley's comet comes close to the sun once about every 76 years. This **false-color** photograph was taken when it last appeared in 1986.

Meteor

As Earth travels through space, it bumps into small rocks and dust left behind from comets. When the rocks and dust hit the top of Earth's **atmosphere,** they burn up, making bright trails in the sky. Astronomers call these trails meteors, or shooting stars. Sometimes, the rocks are too large to burn up. They fall to the ground and are called meteorites.

In the sky
A meteor can look like a bright streak in the sky. It lasts for only a few seconds and then disappears.

Crashing to Earth
About 50 thousand years ago, a large meteorite crashed into the desert in Arizona and made this **crater**.

Asteroid

Astronomers have counted several thousands of asteroids but think there are millions more. Most are too small to be seen from Earth, even with a telescope. The asteroid below is called Gaspra. Its photograph was taken by the Galileo space probe, as it flew past on its way to the planet Jupiter.

Asteroid belt
Most asteroids lie in a ring, or belt, around the sun between the planets Mars and Jupiter.

Star

A star is a huge fiery ball of **gas** that gives out heat and light. The sun is a star and the only one that looks to us like a huge ball in the sky. All the other stars look like pinpoints of light because they are so far away. Stars are not all the same. They are different colors and sizes. Each star also has a lifetime. Once it is born, it will shine steadily for a long time, until it dies.

▶ During its life, a star changes several times. At each stage it looks different.

6 A large star ends its life as a tiny hot ball in a glowing cloud of dust and gas. It is now called a neutron star.

1 A star begins its life inside a large cloud of dust and gas called a nebula.

2 A clump of gas inside the nebula shrinks into a ball, which becomes hotter and starts to glow. This ball is a new star.

Factfile

On a clear night, you can see about 3,000 stars in the sky without using a telescope.

The hottest star that astronomers have found is nearly 40 times hotter than the sun.

*In about five **billion** years, the sun will swell up to a giant star. It may become large enough to swallow up Earth.*

3 The star gives out light and heat steadily for thousands of millions of years, just like the sun does now.

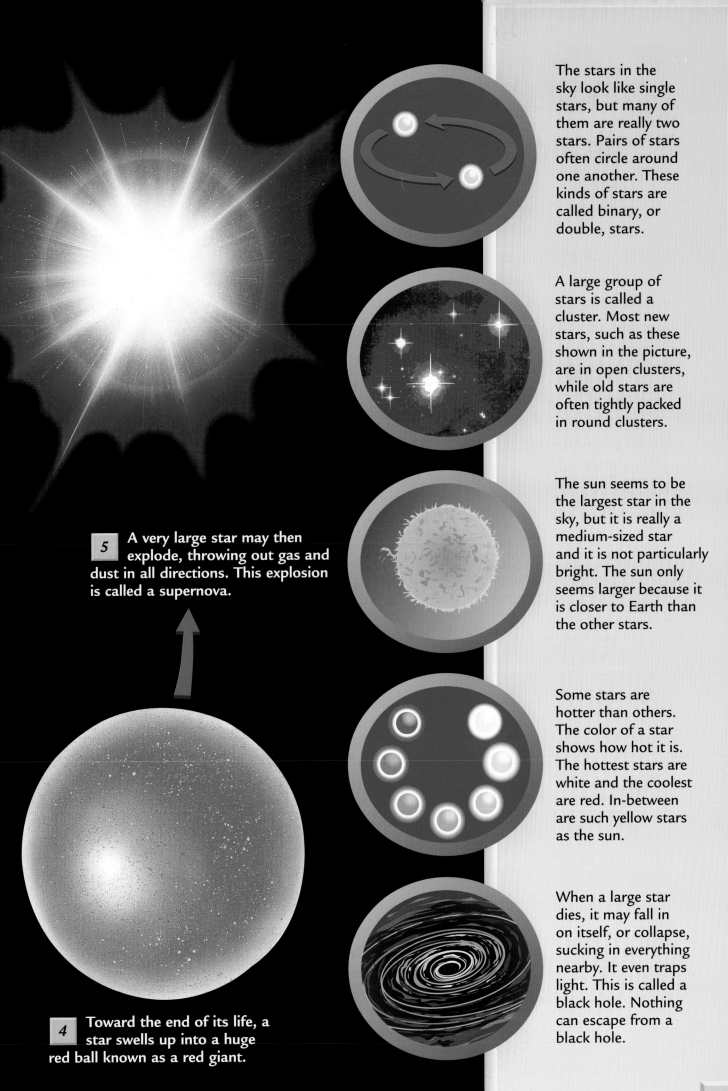

The stars in the sky look like single stars, but many of them are really two stars. Pairs of stars often circle around one another. These kinds of stars are called binary, or double, stars.

A large group of stars is called a cluster. Most new stars, such as these shown in the picture, are in open clusters, while old stars are often tightly packed in round clusters.

The sun seems to be the largest star in the sky, but it is really a medium-sized star and it is not particularly bright. The sun only seems larger because it is closer to Earth than the other stars.

Some stars are hotter than others. The color of a star shows how hot it is. The hottest stars are white and the coolest are red. In-between are such yellow stars as the sun.

When a large star dies, it may fall in on itself, or collapse, sucking in everything nearby. It even traps light. This is called a black hole. Nothing can escape from a black hole.

5 A very large star may then explode, throwing out gas and dust in all directions. This explosion is called a supernova.

4 Toward the end of its life, a star swells up into a huge red ball known as a red giant.

37

Go to Constellations of the southern skies page 40, Star page 36

Constellations
of the northern skies

A constellation is a group of stars that makes a pattern in the sky. Astronomers have counted 88 constellations and given each of them a name. The constellations do not change their shape, but as the night passes, they seem to move across the sky. This happens because Earth is spinning around. The constellations themselves are not really moving. People see different constellations depending on where they live in the world.

▶ This picture shows the main constellations you can see in the northern half of the world. The United States and Canada are in this part of the world.

Fishes

Water Carrier

Androme

Pegasus

Lizard

Dolphin

Deneb

King Cepheus

Ca

Swan

F S

Eagle

Lyre

Lit Be

Milky Way

Drag

Hercules

Serpent Bearer

Northern Crown

Arcturus

Herdsm

Factfile

The brightest star you can see in the northern sky is called Arcturus. It is part of the Herdsman constellation.

The constellations seem to twinkle in the sky. This happens because moving air blurs starlight as it travels to Earth.

The faint Lynx constellation took its name from an animal with sharp eyesight, because you need sharp eyesight to spot it.

Whale

River
Eridanus

m

Rigel

Bull

angle

Orion

Betelgeuse

erseus

Charioteer

Unicorn

affe

Twins

Crab

Lynx

at
ar

Sea
Snake

Hunting
Dogs

erenice's
Hair

Lion

Sextant

Virgin

The constellation Orion was named after a hunter in an ancient story. On Orion's foot is a hot, white star called Rigel. On his shoulder is a cooler, red star named Betelgeuse.

The seven bright, main stars of the Great Bear look more like a saucepan than a bear. Two of these bright stars are called the pointers because they point the way to the **Pole Star**.

The Little Bear also looks like a saucepan but it is not as clear as the Great Bear in the sky. The Pole Star, at the end of the Little Bear's tail, is the brightest star in this constellation.

The Swan is also called the Northern Cross because its stars make the shape of a cross. The brightest star, named Deneb, at the swan's tail, is 60 thousand times brighter than the sun.

Pegasus was named after a magic flying horse in an ancient story. Its brightest stars make it look like a large square in the sky. Pegasus lies next to the Andromeda constellation.

Constellations
of the southern skies

Many constellations, or groups of stars, were named thousands of years ago. Some, such as the Great Dog or the Whale, were named after an animal. Others, such as the Centaur, took their names from creatures or people in ancient stories. In the past, sailors traveling across the ocean used the constellations to find their way. During these long voyages, some new constellations were discovered. They were given names, such as the Sails, after parts of a ship.

▶ This picture shows the main constellations you can see in the southern half of the world. Such places as Australia and most of South America are in this part of the world.

Factfile

Some constellations, such as Orion, can be seen in the southern sky for half of the year and the northern sky for the other half.

The Southern Fish constellation has just one bright star, called Fomalhaut. Long ago, an ancient people thought that Fomalhaut guarded heaven.

The Sea Snake is the largest constellation in the sky.

Sextant

Sea Snake

Sails

Stern

Sirius

Keel

Great
Dog

Unicorn

Painter

Betelgeuse

Dove

Net

Swordfish

Hare

Rigel

Orion

Phenix

River
Eridanus

Whale

nes

The constellation of the Great Dog contains the brightest star in the whole sky. This star is called Sirius, and you can find it at the Dog's head. Sirius is also called the Dog Star.

The Southern Cross is the smallest of all the constellations. It takes its name from its four main stars, which form a cross near the middle of the southern sky. Its simple shape makes it easy to find.

The Centaur is named after a creature that was half man and half horse. Its brightest stars are at its front hooves. The closest star to the sun, called Proxima Centauri, is in this constellation.

The Scorpion is made up mostly of a long line of stars that curl around at its tail. The brightest star in this constellation is called Antares. It is at the middle of the Scorpion's body.

The Archer is a large, bright constellation. It is made up of many stars. New stars are being born all the time in the huge clouds of dust and **gas** that also form part of this constellation.

Go to Astronomer page 8, Star page 36, Telescope page 10

Galaxy

A galaxy is a huge family of stars, dust and **gas** that is held together by **gravity**. The biggest galaxies contain **billions** of stars. Astronomers have counted millions of galaxies in the **universe** using powerful telescopes, but they think there are still many more to be found. Some galaxies shoot out jets of hot gas from their centers, which travel far into space at high speeds.

Milky Way

The sun and Earth lie inside a galaxy called the Milky Way. It is shaped like a spiral, with a bulge in the middle and long, curved arms containing millions of stars. All these stars are moving around the center of the galaxy. You can see part of the Milky Way from Earth. It looks like a faint band of light across the sky.

Nebula

A cloud of gas and dust inside a galaxy is called a nebula. Some nebulae shine brightly, but others are dark. The Horsehead Nebula, above, is a dark cloud shaped like a horse's head. You can see it only because it shows up against the glowing red clouds behind it.

Spiral arm
The spiral arms contain glowing gas clouds where new stars are born.

Sun and Earth
The sun and the Earth lie in one of the spiral arms near the edge of the Milky Way.

Types of galaxies

Galaxies have different shapes. A spiral galaxy has arms curling out from a ball at its center. Some also have a bar across the middle and are called barred spirals. An elliptical galaxy has a round or squashed oval shape. Galaxies without any special shape are called irregular.

Spiral galaxy

Barred spiral galaxy

Elliptical galaxy

Other galaxies

The billions of galaxies in the universe are not spread evenly through space. They lie together in groups called clusters. Sometimes, a large galaxy in the center of one cluster has swallowed up nearby smaller galaxies. The Andromeda Galaxy in this picture is one of the nearest galaxies to the Milky Way and belongs to the same group. It is also about the same size and shape as the Milky Way. The two bright patches are small elliptical galaxies close to the Andromeda Galaxy.

Expanding universe

Astronomers have discovered that distant galaxies are moving away from the Milky Way and also from each other. This proves that the whole universe is expanding, or becoming bigger. In billions of years, the universe may stop expanding. If it does stop, scientists believe that the universe might squash together.

Farther apart

Here the universe has expanded, so the galaxies are farther apart from each other.

Amazing facts

On these pages, you can discover amazing facts about space. You can find out how hot the planets are and how fast they are traveling. You can also learn about the people and animals that have journeyed into space.

How fast are you moving?

The Earth is spinning around, though you do not notice it. The ground you stand on is moving nearly 15 times faster than a car on a highway.

As the Earth spins, it also races around the sun. It travels over 100 times faster than a jumbo jet, though you don't feel this movement at all.

Which planet is...

The hottest?
On Venus, the **temperature** reaches over 860 °F (460 °C) which is about eight times hotter than the hottest temperature ever recorded on Earth.

The coldest?
Pluto receives little heat from the sun. Its temperature sinks to about -387 °F (-220 °C), which is more than twice as cold as the coldest place on the Earth.

Exploring space

Here are some of the most important dates in the history of space travel.

1957

The first satellite, Sputnik 1, was launched by the Soviet Union. This **launch** began the space age.

1961

Yuri Gagarin became the first person to fly in space. He circled Earth in less than two hours.

First space station
Salyut 1 was a Soviet space station launched in 1971. A crew of three people lived and worked in it for three weeks while it circled Earth.

Longest stay on the moon
In 1972, on the last Apollo trip, Eugene Cernan and Harrison Schmitt spent three days on the moon, exploring its surface in their buggy.

Different sizes
is difficult to imagine the sizes of objects in pace because they are so enormous. This picture ompares the sizes of the sun, moon, Earth, and upiter. Imagine the sun is a large beachball...

...then, Jupiter is the size of a tennis ball,...

...Earth is the size of a pea,...

...and the moon is the size of a pinhead.

Which animals have traveled into space?

Dog
In 1957, a dog called Laika became the first living thing to travel in space. Laika proved that it was safe for people to travel in space, too.

Spider
In 1973, two spiders, called Anita and Arabella, lived in the Skylab space station. They showed that spiders could spin webs in space as well as on Earth.

Jellyfish
In 1991, over 2,000 jellyfish were taken on board the space shuttle to see how well they could swim in space. Scientists discovered that the fish became confused and swam in circles instead of straight ahead.

969
uring the Apollo 11 ission, U.S. astronaut Neil rmstrong became the first erson to walk on the moon.

1975
The Apollo and Soyuz **spacecrafts** linked up, beginning the first joint U.S.-Soviet space mission.

1981
The space shuttle Columbia made its first flight ever. It stayed in space for over two days.

1995
The space shuttle Atlantis docked with the Mir space station for the first time.

Glossary

atmosphere A layer of gas that surrounds a planet, star or moon. Earth's atmosphere, called the air, is a mixture of different gases.

billion A number meaning one thousand million, written as 1,000,000,000.

booster rocket A small rocket that is attached to a large space rocket to give extra power at liftoff.

canyon A deep rocky passage with steep sides that lies in between mountains or hills.

core The center of a **planet**, star, or **moon**.

crater A round hole in the ground that is made when a rock from space hits a **planet** or **moon**.

electricity A type of **energy** used to make things such as light and heat, or to make **machines** work.

elliptical Almost round like an oval, or long and thin like a squashed oval.

energy The force that makes things move or work. Some energy can be seen as light, or felt as heat.

engine The part of a **machine**, such as a rocket, that burns **fuel** to make it work or move.

false color Color added to a photograph of an object, such as a galaxy, to make it clearer.

fuel A substance that can be burned to make heat or power.

gas A substance, such as air, that is not solid or liquid. Many gases are invisible and can only be felt if they move.

gravity The force that pulls things toward Earth's surface or toward each other.

laboratory A building or room where scientists work, using special equipment.

lander The part of a spacecraft that lands on the surface of a **planet** or **moon**.

launch To leave Earth on a journey into space.

launch pad The place where rockets take off.

liquid A substance that flows and has no fixed shape, such as water.

lunar lander The part of the Apollo **spacecraft** that landed on the Moon.

machine Something with moving parts that does useful work, such as a **spacecraft**.

moon A natural object in space that travels round a **planet**. A moon is smaller than its planet.

orbit The curved path of an object as it travels in space round a larger object. The planets orbit the sun, and satellites orbit Earth.

oxygen A **gas** in the air that most living things need to breathe to stay alive.

planet A large round object in space, such as Earth, that travels around the sun or another star.

Pole Star The name of the star that lies almost directly above the North Pole, which is the most northern place on Earth.

pollution Unwanted material that spills into the air, sea, or land and damages it.

radio wave An invisible ray that travels through air or space, carrying information that can be made into sounds or pictures.

solid A material that has a firm shape you can feel.

spacecraft Any **vehicle**, such as a rocket or space probe, that flies into space.

temperature A measure of how hot or cold something is.

universe The whole of space and everything in space including the sun, Earth, stars, and galaxies.

vehicle A **machine**, such as a rocket, that moves people or things from place to place.

volcano An opening on the surface of a planet or moon from which ash or hot rock explodes.

weightless Free falling, or floating in space and feeling as if you weigh nothing.

Index

Published in the United States
and Canada by
Two-Can Publishing LLC
234 Nassau Street
Princeton, NJ 08542

www.two-canpublishing.com

© 2000 Two-Can Publishing

For information on Two-Can books and
multimedia, call 1-609-921-6700,
fax 1-609-921-3349, or visit our web site at
http://www.two-canpublishing.com

**Created by
act-two**
346 Old Street
London EC1V 9RB

Disk
Creative Director: William Wharfe
Art Director: Sarah Evans
Project Editor: Lyndall Thomas
Senior Designer: James Evans
Illustrators: Michael Egar, James Evans,
    Richard Harris, James Jarvis
Programmers: Roger Emery,
    Paul Stevens, Martin Sinclair,
    Kirsten Minshall
Consultant: Kevin Johnson, Associate Curator
    of Astronomy and Mathematics,
    Science Museum, London
Production Director: Lorraine Estelle
Production Manager: Katherine Harvey

Book
Art director: Belinda Webster
Managing Editor: Deborah Kespert
Senior Designer: Helen Holmes
Editorial support: Samantha Hilton, Julia Hillyard
Consultant: Doug Millard, Associate Curator
    of Space Technology,
    Science Museum (UK)
Main Illustrations: Gary Bines
    (Blue Chip Illustration)
Computer illustrations: Mel Pickering

'Two-Can' and 'Interfact' are trademarks of
Two-Can Publishing

Two-Can Publishing is a division of
Zenith Entertainment plc,
43-45 Dorset Street, London W1H 4AB

ISBN 1-58728-4731

1 2 3 4 5 6 7 8 9 10 04 03 02 01 00

Photographic credits:
Ancient Art & Architecture Collection: p9tl;
Genesis: p15l; Jet Propulsion Laboratory: p24tr,
p25tr & bl, p29br, p30cl & tr, p33cr & bc; NASA:
p12bl, p25tl, p35bl; Rex Features: p17tr; Robert
Harding: p15tr; Science Photo Library/Martin
Bond p26bl, SPL/Tony Hallas p43cr, SPL/NASA
p21br & p31cr, SPL/Novosti Press Agency p31tr,
SPL/David Nunuk p35tr, SPL/Roger Ressmeyer-
Starlight p27br, SPL/Royal Greenwich
Observatory p9br, SPL/Royal Observatory
Edinburgh p34br & p42tr, SPL/John Sanford
p35cr, SPL/Robin Scagell p10br; Tony Stone
Images: p11t, p26bl; Zefa: p8cl.

Printed in Hong Kong

*T*roubleshooting tips

System requirements

The Space disk will work on most Windows or Apple Macintosh computers. To check that it will run on yours, please read the minimum specifications below.

Windows

486DX2/66Mhz PC with Windows version 3.1, 3.11, 95 or 98; VGA color monitor; SoundBlaster-compatible soundcard; 8Mb RAM (16Mb RAM recommended with Windows 95; 24 Mb recommended with Windows 98).

Macintosh

Apple Macintosh with 68020 processor (or Power Macintosh), system 7.0 (or later) and 16Mb of RAM (24 Mb with Power Macintosh).

Quick fixes

To get the most out of your Space disk, please check:
1. Your monitor is set to 640 x 480 and 256 colors.
2. You have the Arial font (Windows users) installed in your fonts folder.
3. You have no other applications open.

Read me file

If you have a problem with your Space disk, be sure to check the Read me file. To open this, click on the Read me icon which you will find next to the Space icon. If you are using Windows 95 or 98, you will need to open the Read me file using Windows Explorer.

Helpline

If you come across a problem loading or running the Space disk, you should find the solution here. If you still cannot solve your problem, call the helpline at 1-609-921-6700. Remember to get permission from the person who pays the bill before you use the phone.

CHECK OUT THE WHOLE INTERFACT RANGE

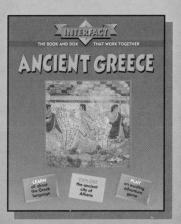

There is a huge range of INTERFACT titles to choose from. Watch out for new titles too!